shelter cats

cats

edwena's home

julia grunwell

authorHOUSE®

AuthorHouse™
1663 Liberty Drive
Bloomington, IN 47403
www.authorhouse.com
Phone: 1 (800) 839-8640

Published by AuthorHouse 09/27/2018

ISBN: 978-1-5462-6042-4 (sc)
ISBN: 978-1-5462-6041-7 (e)

Library of Congress Control Number: 2018911078

Print information available on the last page.

*Any people depicted in stock imagery provided by Getty Images are
models, and such images are being used for illustrative purposes only.
Certain stock imagery © Getty Images.*

This book is printed on acid-free paper.

dedication

For all those kittens out there without a home, may all your kitty wishes come true.

chapter one

Un-cat-isfactory Conditions

"Great. Another shelter."

Edwena looked curiously around her new home. Cats, cats, and more cats. Edwena had hoped, although not expected, that maybe she would be the only cat in this shelter. No one to bother her, no one to compete with. Here at Kitty Wishes, there were cats in cages above, below, and on either side of Edwena. There were even some cats outside of cages!

"Ugh! I've been here three hours and my fur is a mess. I've been poked and prodded, and it's so noisy, I need rest!" she yelled furiously.

All the cats stopped what they were doing and stared at her. Then, muttering to themselves, they went back to their business. Edwena curled up in the corner of her cage, feeling humiliated, but refusing to show it.

Edwena had a long history of being brushed aside. Her first family of two-leggers seemed kind enough. They snuggled with her in their mansion. They fed her shrimp and tuna fish right out of the can. She played hide-and-seek in their treehouse. She even rode in a mini boat in their pool. Life was good.

As Edwena grew, her two-leggers started leaving her behind more and more often. They began to fill her food bowl to the brim with dry cat food every few days. No more shrimp and tuna. When Edwena would hide in the treehouse, she started to realize that no one ever came to look for her anymore. She tried to snuggle, but the two-leggers didn't seem interested. She tried to look adorable in the mini boat, but Edwena found that she no longer fit in the kitten-sized yacht. Her two-leggers had lost interest in Edwena.

One morning, her two-leggers took Edwena on a trip. Edwena thought, "Yay! Things are back to normal. They remember me." But then they pulled up in front of a place with a sign that read *Kitten Kaboodle Shelter*. Edwena's excitement vanished.

"Oh no," she thought, as something dawned on her. Edwena was going to be put in a shelter.

chapter two

The Mouse Trap

Edwena's first days at the shelter weren't too bad. She was fed every day, was able to take naps whenever she wanted, and had some nice neighbors. Every couple of days, someone would come into the shelter to look for a cat to take home. At first, Edwena would go to the front of her cage in excitement, purring loudly, batting her eyelashes, and flicking her tail. Some two-leggers would pause in front of her cage and say, "Aww, how cute! Maybe we should adopt her," but they would always move on.

Days turned into weeks, and weeks turned into months. When two-leggers came in looking for a pet to take home, Edwena didn't bother purring for them. She stopped batting her eyelashes. She stopped flicking her tail. Eventually, Edwena just curled up in the back of her cage and stayed there when pet-seekers peered in.

"Why even bother trying to get noticed?" she thought. "They are just going to choose one of the other cats anyway." One day, Edwena was curling up in the back of her cage, burying her ears in her paws to muffle the sounds of the two-leggers finding their new pets all around her. Unexpectedly on that particular day, someone actually hand-picked Edwena. A white-haired two-legger holding a long curved wooden stick that seemed to help him walk entered the shelter. He walked past the energetic kittens. He walked past the fluffy Persians. And he came to a stop in front of Edwena's cage and pointed.

"I'll take that one. Is it free?" he said gruffly.

And so began Edwena's new life.

Edwena's time at the white-haired two-legger's house was mostly spent in the basement. It wasn't all bad at first, though. When Edwena got there, she was very hungry. She heard a faint snuffling sound and glanced up. All of a sudden, a mouse appeared, holding some cheese. The mouse offered her some cheese to share.

Over the next few days, Edwena found friendship with the many tiny mice that lived in the otherwise lonely basement. Sometimes they would sneak out together in search of food. Other times, they just huddled together in the corner near the furnace to keep warm. Companionship felt good to Edwena.

Every once in a while, the white-haired two-legger would come down the stairs, walk around to all the corners, and grumble something about "missing cheese" and "pesky rodents." Then he would turn to Edwena and say something like, "Useless little furball you are, cat. I thought your kind ate mice!"

One day, as the two-legger turned to go up the stairs, Edwena tried to snuggle up against his leg. He shook her off immediately and slammed the door in her face. From the other side of the door, Edwena heard, "Start getting rid of mice, or I'll get rid of you!" At that moment, Edwena realized with a jolt why she was brought to this home in the first place. It wasn't because she was adorable or snuggly or even talented. She was adopted to be a hunter. And there was no way she could take on that role when her new (only) friends were meant to be her prey.

Upon realizing the expectation that the two-legger had for her, Edwena hastened to the back of the old washing machine in the darkest part of the basement, where the mice lived. She pleaded with them to leave. "Go find somewhere else to live, or he's going to find a way to get rid of you!" Edwena cautioned the rodents.

The mice didn't seem concerned, though. They were used to being chased, swatted, trapped, and tricked. So, Edwena knew that it was *she* who would have to flee. She said a tearful farewell to her new friends, they wished each other luck, and Edwena squeezed out through a hole that the mice had chewed in the basement door. Edwena had made a difficult decision in order to be a good friend. Because of that choice, Edwena found herself more alone than ever.

chapter three

The Cat's Out of the Bag!

For a week, Edwena roamed around trying to find somewhere else to live. When Edwena came across an abandoned park as she wandered, she thought, "I could stay here." Weeks passed as she spent her days under the slide in the shade and her nights in the tunnel, shielded from the wind and the foxes that sometimes appeared at night. Edwena moped around the playground like this, feeling sorry for herself, until a group of small two-leggers came to the playground and picked up Edwena and took her home with them.

A day later Edwena went to the vet for the

first time in a while. When they got there Edwena got shots, had some fleas removed, and was given vitamins. Most remarkably, she could not remember a time when she had felt (or smelled) as good as she did after the luxurious bath she received there.

Just as Edwena began to have hope for this new living situation, she overheard the father of the little two-leggers telling the doctor, between sneezes and nose blows, that he felt so guilty about dropping Edwena off like this. "My kids -- ACHOO! -- will be so upset, but -- ACHOO! -- we just can't keep the poor girl."

He waved to Edwena and wished her good luck as the veterinarian scooped her up and carried her to a cage in a back room. Edwena heard the honking sound of the father's nose fade out as the door to the back room closed softly. Faster than Father Two-legger could say, "Achoo!", Edwena understood that she was once again a shelter cat.

In the vet's shelter it was just Edwena and a lopsided guinea pig with a weird bald patch in the middle of her forehead.

The guinea pig introduced herself as Ginny, so Edwena told Ginny her name. In the time Edwena spent in the shelter no other animals came in, except for a brightly colored, annoying parrot. This flying heap of feathers, named Repeat, was certainly more company than Edwena knew what to do with.

Repeat did not seem to have a very extensive vocabulary, mostly speaking in idioms, rhymes, and puns, but that did not stop him from talking. All. The. Time. When he first arrived, early one morning, Ginny and Edwena tried to befriend the colorful bird. He spent the next hour squawking, "Ginny guinea pig!" and "The cat's out of the bag!" Edwena was not amused.

For a month Edwena lived there with Repeat and Ginny. She slowly began to feel like she had friends again. Edwena laughed with Ginny, imitated Repeat, and played tricks on the vet with both of them. Edwena was shocked to find out that she felt as if Ginny and Repeat were her family.

One morning, Edwena returned from her relaxing bath and nail clipping to find that Ginny and Repeat were not around. Figuring they were probably getting groomed themselves, Edwena climbed into her cage and settled in for a nap. When she awoke, her friends were still not in their cages. Edwena sat up with a jolt, padded across her cage, and as she was about to call out for Ginny, she felt something crinkle under her paw. She lifted her foot to find a crumpled piece of a wrapper from one of Ginny's treats. Scratched into the ink was a message that read:

Edwena,

> *We won't be coming back. We can't live in the shelter any more. We need to spread our wings (and claws). Please forgive us for leaving without you. Good luck!*

Ginny + Repeat

Edwena could not believe what she was reading. Her friends - her *family* - had left her behind. She had no warning, no idea that this was coming. Ginny and Repeat had plotted and planned behind Edwena's back. The hope and excitement she had previously felt at having friends to live with transformed into betrayal and sadness.

For hours Edwena sprawled in the corner of her cage, her tummy feeling sick, reading the note over and over until the words blurred and she fell asleep. At nighttime Edwena awoke, wishing this was all a bad dream, and she looked up hoping she would see Ginny and Repeat in their cages, squeaking and squawking. But in her heart, she knew they were gone for good.

What Edwena heard next made it impossible for her to sleep that night. The kind veterinarian walked past her cage, talking into her cell phone:

"I've looked everywhere! The guinea pig and parrot are not here. They must have gotten out the back door when today's medicine delivery arrived," the vet told whoever was on the other end of the line. "I'm already having trouble keeping up with the bills. I can't pay to keep the shelter open for just one cat. Is it OK if I drop her off to your location in the morning?"

After a sleepless night, Edwena was once again packed in a crate and taken to another temporary home. The veterinarian's car shook and rattled with every bump in the road during the long drive to Edwena's next stop. As the car finally slowed to a stop, Edwena blinked away tears and licked her paws as she spotted the *Kitty Wishes* sign. The crate began to move toward a little wooden building with a front porch swing and yellow shutters.

"Here we go again," griped Edwena.

chapter four

Yoo-hoo Do You Think You Are?

Edwena decided she would try to blend in with the scenery at Kitty Wishes. She did not want to be noticed. She did not want to make friends. She did not want to be adopted. She just wanted to be left alone. It was *her* own 'Kitty Wish'.

Unfortunately, none of the other cats in the shelter would allow this wish to come true. They were always saying hello, singing, having loud conversations around her, and asking more questions than Edwena wanted to answer.

"Where did you live before this?" one wanted to know.

"Do you like two-leggers?" another inquired.

"How do you get your tail to flick like that?" the nosy calico named Yoo-hoo asked.

Edwena usually responded to these questions with a roll of her eyes and a little hiss. Most of the other cats at Kitty Wishes quickly got the hint. The calico seemed to be oblivious to the message Edwena was sending. Yoo-hoo was in the cage next to Edwena's, and he never stopped trying to strike up a conversation.

Around 5:00 in the morning Edwena heard a rustling sound and groggily opened her eyes. She looked around and quickly found the source of the noise. In the cage next to her Yoo-hoo was bouncing energetically off the cage walls. When Yoo-hoo

noticed Edwena he said, "Oh good you're awake! I have really exciting news."

Yoo-hoo went on to say, "The lock on my cage is broken. I need to move into your cage temporarily."

"What did you say?" Edwena rubbed the sleep from her eyes, barely able to process what the crazy calico was saying to her in these early morning hours.

"Isn't that great?! We're going to be roomies!" Yoo-hoo announced, seeming not to notice Edwena's eye rolling at the news. Edwena silently rolled her eyes right back to bed and pretended to fall back to sleep. But this news had sent her into fits of worry.

Roomies?! Edwena thought. *This will be a disaster! Even if I wanted the company (which I don't!), anyone who lives with me will surely head for the hills in no time. Not to mention, with this crazy cat, I'll never get any sleep around here.*

Edwena worried herself back to sleep until she was awakened by the unlatching of her cage door. Sure enough, a two-legger was lifting Yoo-hoo right into Edwena's space. As the two-legger locked the cage door and walked away, Yoo-hoo began to dart all around the cage, exploring every identical, empty corner.

"Wow! It sure is neat and tidy in here!" Yoo-hoo complimented Edwena.

"Yeah, and make sure you keep it that way too. How long are you staying anyway?" Edwena snapped.

"Probably only a couple of days, but if we're lucky, maybe they won't EVER be able to fix my cage!" the oblivious calico replied. "Oh, we're just going to have the BEST time!"

With a grunt, Edwena promptly nosed her bed to the opposite side of the cage, as far away from Yoo-hoo as possible. "It's time for my mid-morning nap," grumbled Edwena, as she haughtily raised her tail high in the air before flopping down on her bed once again.

For the next couple of days (endless days, in Edwena's opinion), Edwena would awaken from each of her daily naps to Yoo-hoo peppering her with questions.

"Did you sleep ok?"

"Did you have any dreams?"

"Do you believe in soulmates?"

"Why do you think the food here tastes like pickle juice?"

Every night after the two-legger turned out the lights for bedtime, Edwena heard Yoo-hoo's slightly less energetic voice whisper, "Nighty-night! Sleep tight. Don't let the shelter fleas bite!" Although she would never admit it to Yoo-hoo, after a few nights, Edwena started to mouth along with Yoo-hoo's goodnight message as she yawned and settled into her cozy bed. Sometimes it wasn't so bad at nighttime to have someone close by and remember she isn't always alone.

Finally, the big day came: Yoo-hoo's moving day. Edwena woke up to find a downcast Yoo-hoo walking the corners of her cage one last time.

"Are you all packed and ready?" Edwena questioned him, not wanting to seem too interested in Yoo-hoo's living arrangements.

"Yup and ready to go to home sweet home," answered Yoo-hoo while trying to sound upbeat, cheerful, and perky. It was clear to Edwena that Yoo-hoo was faking his usual blinding smile, and the quiver in his voice revealed a sadness that the calico had never shown before.

Surprised by the fact that she actually felt a bit sad herself, Edwena nudged Yoo-hoo with her tail and teased, "Knowing you, I'm sure you'll find a way to break that cage door again in no time. I'll probably have to make room for you in here again." She pretended to be annoyed at the thought, but the gesture made Yoo-hoo brighten up and smile a bit of his sparkly grin.

chapter five

Thunder Booms and Friendship Blooms

"Feeding time! Feeding time!" a shrill-voiced two-legger called out, awakening Edwena and the other cats from their slumber. For most of the cats this was the best time of the day, but for Edwena it was the worst. She hated getting up early, fighting for space at the food bowl, and not being able to eat all the food she wanted.

This morning, however, Edwena crawled out of her cage feeling more cheerful than usual. She called good morning to a fat black and white cat and hummed on her way to the food bowl.

Edwena tried to squeeze into a small spot between two cats but she was unsuccessful. She chose a different spot on the other side of the bowl and tried to wiggle her way through so she could reach the mixture of tuna and dry cat food, as its aroma was filling her nostrils. A shaggy-haired white cat nudged Edwena with her hind quarters hard enough to knock her back on her own backside. She heard this cat whisper to the rest of the feeders, "Do you believe that new one? She thinks she gets first dibs on feeding time!" The cats around the bowl laughed through their munching. They were all laughing at Edwena.

"Mouse! Mouse!" called out a voice from somewhere near the back door.

The hungry, laughing cats seemed to turn without

a thought and pounce toward the back hallway. Suddenly, Edwena noticed Yoo-hoo appearing from the crowd of hunters and walking toward her. "Well, that's one way to clear a food bowl!" he said with a sly smile. "Eat up before they realize there is no rodent dessert back there."

"You did that … for me?" Edwena wondered aloud.

"Why not?" answered Yoo-hoo. "The other cats weren't letting you have any food and that's not fair. After all, that's what friends do for each other! Right?"

At that moment, Edwena realized that she wasn't the only cat in the shelter who didn't have much experience with having friends. The tuna and dry cat food tasted like heaven that morning.

In the days that followed, Edwena and Yoo-hoo began spending more time together. They schemed to figure out ways to get a turn at the food bowl each morning. They cracked inside jokes about the rude cats that tried to nudge them out of the way. Soon they both began to see that they had a lot in common. They had both managed to stay virtually friendless as they bounced from shelter to shelter. The two of them had also both spent time in families of two-leggers, and they even felt comfortable enough to admit that they felt sad and lonely sometimes, even though neither let it show very often.

Nighttime fell as the two-legger came in and

turned out the light. The muffled sounds of thunder could be heard in the distance, a sign that a storm was approaching. At midnight Edwena woke to a faint whimpering sound from Yoo-hoo's cage. She peered into his cage finding him curled up in the corner, rocking back and forth.

"Yoo-hoo?" Edwena said in a small voice. "Are you okay?" A crash of thunder rattled all the cages in the room.

"I'm terrified of thunderstorms," answered Yoo-hoo, shakily getting to his feet and crossing his cage toward Edwena. A flash of lightning lit up the room, and Edwena could see that Yoo-hoo had been crying. A loud boom of thunder sent Yoo-hoo scurrying back across his cage.

"Yoo-hoo! Come back here. You can lay right here," suggested Edwena. She herself stretched out along the perimeter of the side of her cage that touched Yoo-hoo's cage.

"Did I ever tell you that story about the cat who rode a dinosaur? Or the one about the cat who defeated a dragon?" Edwena rambled as she tried to comfort Yoo-hoo.

"I love dinosaurs! Tell me that one," Yoo-hoo began to feel calmer and safer already.

Edwena stayed awake and told Yoo-hoo one make believe story after another until he yawned one big yawn and settled into a deep sleep.

"Nighty night," Edwena whispered, "sleep tight. Don't let the shelter fleas bite." She, too, fell into a relaxing slumber. It felt good to feel good.

chapter six

The Move

In the morning, Edwena heard the sound of a creaky door swinging open. She looked to her right and saw an empty hallway. When she looked to her left, she saw a big group of two-leggers strolling toward her.

"Yoo-hoo! Yoo-hoo! Wake up! Wake up!" Edwena yelped.

Like a rocket, Yoo-hoo shot up from his bed and crossed his cage.

"What? What's wrong?" he asked Edwena.

"Look," she replied somberly as she nodded her head toward the two-leggers who were now entering the room.

All around the room, confused and nervous cats were wriggling in the hands of the two-leggers who were plucking them from their cages. Hissing and high-pitched meowing filled the air as the now wide awake felines were carried out through the door at the end of the hall.

"Where does that door lead?" Edwena wondered aloud.

She didn't receive an answer, for obvious reasons, but Edwena began to draw her own conclusions. If her past was any indication, that door led to the truck that would take her to some new place once again. Probably a place filled with new cats and new people and new food. This was a place Edwena knew well, even though she had never been there before.

What Edwena didn't understand, though, was the feeling that was welling up in her belly. The thought of going to another new place made her feel like everything inside her was twisting and turning. She had never felt this way before, despite all of the moves she had gone through. What was this feeling, and why did it hurt so badly?

"It's friendship," Yoo-hoo replied.

Edwena hadn't even realized she had been worrying aloud for all - especially Yoo-hoo - to hear.

"What?" Edwena tried to subtly lick away the tears that had begun to spill through her whiskers.

"I don't want to go somewhere without you,

Edwena. And you don't want to go without me either!" Yoo-hoo wisely went on. "Whatever is going on right now, promise we will find a way to stick together."

Edwena smiled a worried smirk. "You are the most clever cat I've ever had as a friend, Yoo-hoo. Remember that."

She had just enough time to give Yoo-hoo a gentle flick of her tail when the sounds of two-leggers unlatching their cages suddenly made the moment all too real. A pleasant-looking two-legger with a kind expression reached in Edwena's cage and gently lifted her out. She squirmed at first, but then the two-legger adjusted her grip on Edwena so she wouldn't work her way out of her hands.

Edwena was carried out of the hallway that she lived in, the hallway where she had made her first friend. The two-legger turned to the right and walked down the hall until she reached the door that Edwena had been eyeing suspiciously. Edwena looked worriedly over her shoulder at Yoo-hoo who was being carried in the arms of a burly, tall two-legger. Edwena faced front once again as the two-legger opened the swinging door. She closed her eyes tight and drew up the strength she would need to face yet another shakeup in her ever-changing life.

Seconds later, the two-legger exclaimed, "Here you are, kitty! Home sweet home!" She placed

Edwena on the floor, where Yoo-hoo quickly caught up to her. Even Yoo-hoo found himself speechless as the two friends walked into a room that looked like nothing they had ever seen before. It was a kitty paradise! As they glanced around wide-eyed at the scratching posts, glass cages, and comfortable, shaggy rugs, Edwena and Yoo-hoo began to realize that they had not been headed for a separation after all. In fact, they soon discovered that they were going to live *together* here.

"It sure seems like the cats will have plenty of room for exercise and relaxing in this new room," one of the uniformed two-leggers remarked to the others. "We were lucky to receive that donation to help us pay for this renovation."

But Edwena and Yoo-hoo really felt like the lucky ones. They explored their new surroundings and found that they would be sharing one of the spacious and comfortable glass cages with each other and two other friendly felines: Lotus and Palmer.

Edwena had never been so happy, and she didn't even try to hide it. She bounced from one cat perch to another, chasing Yoo-hoo and their new friends, grateful that she had ended up at Kitty Wishes. This was sure to be the *purr*-fect new home for Edwena.

edwena's new family

Edwena

Yoo-hoo

Lotus

Palmer

about the illustrator

Colleen Harrison has liked art since she was a kid. She always wanted to draw more. Growing up she had a dog named Heidi. Now as an adult she has eight cats. Colleen has volunteered at the local cat shelter for almost twelve years! She introduced the author to the shelter cats who inspired this story. She did not train as an artist but never gave up her love for art.

about the author

Julia Grunwell is a kitten fanatic! She sees a lot of herself in Edwena. When she is not writing stories about cats, she is getting inspired by visiting her local cat rescue shelter. She lives in Bucks County, Pennsylvania with her parents and her two older sisters, Caroline and Elizabeth. Her favorite authors include J.K. Rowling and Ridley Pearson. She loves to draw, read, and travel with her family. An animal lover, Julia also loves meeting new dogs, bunnies, and horses.

acknowledgments

Mom-mom and Pop-pop,
for encouraging my love of writing

Mrs Z., for helping my dreams turn into a book

Mrs Harrison, for opening my world to cats

My mom, for everything

96490000R00029

Made in the USA
Middletown, DE
30 October 2018